WE LIKE FEELINGS.
WE ARE SERIOUS.

WE LIKE FEELINGS. WE ARE SERIOUS.

JULIE McISAAC

A Buckrider Book

Buckrider Books is an imprint of Wolsak and Wynn Publishers.

Cover and interior design: Natalie Olsen, Kisscut Design
Cover image © Nabi Tang
Author photograph: Sean Springer
Typeset in Sina Nova by Hoftype
Printed by Coach House Printing Company Toronto, Canada

The publisher gratefully acknowledges the support of the Canada Council for the Arts, the Ontario Arts Council and the Government of Canada.

Buckrider Books
280 James Street North
Hamilton, Ontario
Canada L8R 2L3

Library and Archives Canada Cataloguing in Publication
McIsaac, Julie, author
We like feelings. We are serious. / Julie McIsaac.
Poems.
ISBN 978-1-928088-69-1 (softcover)
I. Title.
PS8625.I82W3 2018   C811'.6   C2018-903871-3

To Sean.
Thank you for sharing your life with me.

CONTENTS

STATEMENT OF POETICS

Every loss I have ever felt has registered in my brain, marked my body, and influenced all of my relationships. I know that you feel the same way. Please believe me, I want sincerity most of all; however, I am saddened and frustrated to find that I, too, am tyrannized by irony.

WE LIKE FEELINGS. WE ARE SERIOUS.

Our fathers all killed themselves, and then we were left with
their record collections, covers turning to mould, stored in crates,
stacked incorrectly; towers of vinyl teetering with age. We added
to this collection over time, visiting used record stores and thrift
shops because we considered this a hobby. We spent what little
money we had on tattoos of elephants or handguns: ironic signs
that signified nothing. If people asked us what they meant, we got
angry. "It don't mean nothin'!" we'd say.

We talked in clipped sentences, calling and answering to trivial
questions about obscure bands that formed obscure links to other
obscure bands. Around this time, we stopped listening to music.
We stopped eating flesh, stopped drinking blood. We stopped
having sex, even oral sex. We stopped fingering. Next went hand
jobs, rim jobs and mutual masturbation. Then, even regular
masturbation. Some of us stopped kissing. ("Not me!" cried a little
one of us from the back. "I never stopped kissing!") We walked
around with razor blades stored in our cheeks so that if we smiled
they'd cut us and we'd bleed so this way we didn't smile.

Now, the little one of us in the back cries out that we are all a
bunch of motherfuckers. ("Get your hands in the air!" the little
one of us in the back yells. "We've come for your daughters, but
we'll settle for your scalps!")

And we realized that it was time for our fathers to die again.
So we formed factions. Out of this was formed Enemy.

Enemy says: *We had a goatee this morning, but we could tell that you were a moustache crowd, so we shaved.*

Enemy says: *I miss the good old days. Whatever happened to our fathers? Let's hold an event at a local pub and read all their suicide notes aloud.*

But Enemy knows THEY ALL LEFT THE SAME NOTE!
And beer ain't cheap, even at the local.

Enemy says: *I'll get you back next time,* then snores really loud for all of eternity.

Enemy says: *Genet? Not sure . . .*
Neither are we! Stop talking like us, Enemy!

Enemy says: *Swift reflexes are key.*
And we think about it.

Enemy says: *Beer makes you fat.*

One day Enemy will scream: *I want to have oral sex with you all night long! What does* hermeneutic *mean? If you tell me, I promise not to laugh!*

Enemy will cry to the heavens, fists clenched and pumping:
I've said too much. I've listened too little. All I've lost . . . I am such a fool.

We are not waiting for that day. Our story is a long one:
We kicked down the tower of song and built a structure of
feelings. A bungalow. We're all sitting in it now, talking about our
feelings. We kiss each other's teeth with our lips. We gash each
other's lips with our teeth. We spend what little money we have
on baseball bats and we hit each other over the head with them,
then we hit ourselves over the head with them. Then we use them
to destroy all the record players just because we feel like it.

If someone calls it "making love," then we refuse to have sex with
them. We are having sloppy sex with a guy who isn't really our
boyfriend. We are waiting for the day he turns into a woman.
We shave off all our pubic hair so our cocks and cunts can really
be out in the open. We kneel down and kiss every toe on every
foot of every pro-sex feminist who ever lived. We wrap our supple
lips around cocks and work them down to the backs of our throats
against the warm beds that are our velvet tongues. After, these
tongues flicker against bloated, throbbing clitorises that ache with
their own pulse, then tremble against the warmth of a wet mouth.
We / Dig / Penetration.
We are fingering ourselves right now.

We have a standing army. We are ready to fight wars against our
oppressors, or against those who say "fewer" when they mean to
say "less." (But our mothers used to call our rain gear "unberellas"
and we know that they were geniuses.) We are all working very
hard to get good jobs for all the women so they can buy just as
much vacation as the men. We get drunk. Often. We're drunk
right now! Even those of us who are driving!

We are trying to invent the cigarette that isn't bad for you.
We are inventing an anti-wrinkle cream that makes you feel high
on cocaine. There's no comedown. Only fewer wrinkles.

We end the present tale by taking the razor blades out of our
mouths and cutting deep, rectangular patches in our skin,
and then tearing them from our breasts, our thighs, our asses
("You're all a bunch of asses!" the little one of us cries), our arms
and our bellies. We stick the thick cuts of skin to invisible walls.
They are held there by their bloody side. We watch them. It is a
miracle! They / Keep / On / Bleeding.

YOUNG LOVE IN THE POST-ACTIVISM ERA

I decided to take the subway to his house even though it was
his turn to come to mine. The subway car that I got into was full,
with only one small space left for me. Once I was on the subway,
two police officers pushed their way into the same car. They
had curly white cords coming out of their ears. I was squished
between them and I thought I was going to start hyperventilating
so I decided to get off at the next stop even though it wasn't mine
and so when the subway stopped and the doors opened I asked
them to move. They both leaned about one and a half millimetres
to either side. I squeezed between them and almost fell onto the
platform. I am the only person on the platform.

The subway left and then

two minutes later an announcement said

that the green line was out of service.

Fucking pigs.

They were hanging out in the backroom of the organic grocery store, drinking fair-trade coffee and she asked him what he thought about weapons in Iraq and he said "you're beautiful" and she smiled because to her that was the absolute right answer.

On the bus everyone stands at the front and no one sits at the back so I squeezed through everyone and then sat down. And then all of a sudden, as soon as I sat down, I started feeling stressed out for no good reason. Like I forgot something. I feel like I never should have left my house. I know that I wore the wrong shoes.

That was the exact moment when

I realized that

I am lonely.

They took the bus downtown and when they arrived they sat next to a giant fountain. They threw pennies in and made wishes. Then they clipped their hair and planted it in the dirty weeds that sprouted through the concrete next to where the fountain was built. They made more wishes. They thought *future*. She said nothing.

From the back of the bus I saw this old man in the front get up from his seat and make his way to the rear doors. The man looked like a fit, adventurous seventy-year-old, like Gene Hackman or Harrison Ford. He was wearing an all-black outfit that looked like a SWAT team uniform. He had a cellphone in his breast pocket that was so big it looked like a walkie-talkie. When the bus stopped, instead of just waving his hand under the sensor to open the back door, he dropped his right foot back and then did a karate chop that landed just in front of the yellow strip.

The doors opened;

he stood up straight

and left the bus.

They finally realized that originality is what drives the capitalist economy. If everyone strove to just fit in, then this oppressive system would end. "More of the same!" they cried in the streets. "We want more of the same!"

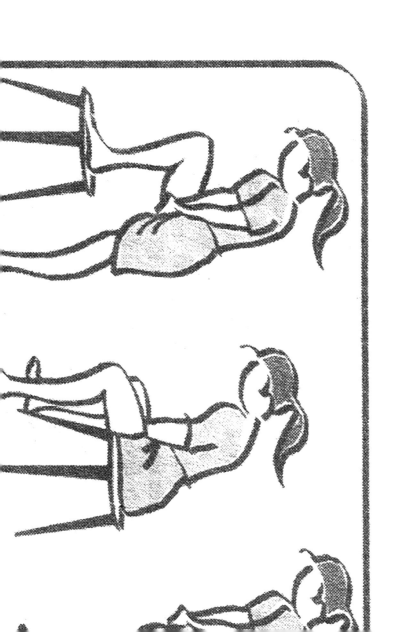

I don't know but I just get this feeling like he's not really that interested in me anymore. He said he was going to call me on Thursday and then he didn't. So I thought that might mean he was blowing me off but I also wanted to give him the benefit of the doubt and thought that maybe something happened or maybe I was supposed to call him and it was all just a big misunderstanding. But then by ten-thirty Friday night when he still hadn't called, I called him and then I left a message and I always sound like such an asshole on answering machines because I get nervous, especially since he has one of those old-fashioned machines and he might be screening his calls and secretly listening to everything that I say as I say it and maybe his roommates are there too. So I think that my voice was shaking a little when I called him and then I left him the message and when I hung up I said to myself *That is it! That relationship is over because you are so weird, you are so fucking weird and you leave the weirdest phone messages.* But then at midnight he called me back, never said anything about the fact that he was supposed to call me on Thursday and I didn't bring it up either because it was just so nice to finally talk to him. I told him we could get together for coffee this weekend, as long as I'm not too busy. But now I'm taking the bus to his house at night even though he's the one with the car,

which is stupid

and I know that

but I guess I wasn't so busy after all.

I could show him the poem about the cops because it's kind of tough and I bet he'd like it and he'd see a new side of me, but then again, I know what he'll say. He'll say, "I'm sorry I ever hurt you, Baby, but it was me that I was mad at. I never meant to be a player. I want to build a relationship, I really do, but I'm frightened. Not of you, but of me, of us and how good it could really be. You know (chuckle) it's funny, but sometimes it's being happy that I'm most afraid of. But I see that I was wrong and I want to try, I want to change and make it work, even though I'm scared. Let's do this together. Will you help me be a better person, even after all I've done to you?"

And then after that

he'll play guitar some more.

They walked toward the wall of riot police. They lay down in front of the blockade and made love on top of the Canadian flag. They orgasmed simultaneously. They dropped out of university together, on the same day. They moved to an island that no one else had ever heard of before. They ate fish and they caught the fish using only a spear that they whittled out of a tree branch using a nail file that she'd forgotten she had that she found at the bottom of her purse. They seasoned the fish with the salt of the earth. When they ate together, without utensils, he would look at her and smile and say, "Mmm, salt of the earth."

It is cold, but it has been colder. I made the decision to switch from Earl Grey to chai. For good. I've also been doing an increasingly good job of remembering to floss every night before bed. I also have a Post-it Note stuck to my computer monitor that says DECIDE WHAT TO DO WITH THE REST OF YOUR LIFE, and usually when I write things in places where I see them then I actually remember to get them done.

Things are really looking up,

as you may have noticed.

Things are really happening.

YOUNG FEMINISTS IN THE ARCHIVE ERA

Journal
Australian Feminist Studies ›
Volume 32, 2017 - Issue 91-92: Archives and New Modes of Feminist Research

Articles

Feminist Archiving [*a manifesto continued*]: Skilling for Activism and Organising

Jenna Ashton ✉

Pages 126-149 | Published online: 30 Aug 2017

66 Download citation   🔗 https://doi.org/10.1080/08164649.2017.1357010   ⟳ Check for updates

🖹 Full Article   🖻 Figures & data   🖉 References   66 Citations   📊 Metrics   🔓 Reprints & Permissions   Get access

ABSTRACT

This article outlines the potential of a model of material and digital feminist archiving that sits within a wider context of feminist activism and organising. It argues that feminist archiving is a circular process of creating the society we want to be evidenced, and contributes to the skilling

People also read

Article

Stains and Remains:

○ ○ ○ 📄 Guide to the Kathleen Hanna ×
← → C ⊕ dlib.nyu.edu/findingaids/html/fales/hanna/
See all finding aids in this repository

Print / View Finding Aid as Single Page

Click here to request materials using your Special Collections Research Account

TheFales Library &Special Collections

Guide to the Kathleen Hanna Papers, 1988-2015 MSS.271

Fales Library and Special Collections
Elmer Holmes Bobst Library
70 Washington Square South
3rd Floor
New York, NY 10012
Phone: (212) 998-2596
fales.library@nyu.edu

Fales Library and Special Collections
Collection processed by Liza Harrell-Edge, 2011
This finding aid was produced using ArchivesSpace on August 25, 2017
Finding aid written in English
Reprocessed by Rachel Corbman Zine abstracts added by Nik Dragovic Record edited by Rachel Searcy to reflect 2015 accretion Updated by Jacqueline Rider to reflect incorporation of video preservation master and sub-master files Updated by Megan O'Shea to prepare artwork being sent to offsite art storage in September 2017 , March 20132013 , October 2016 , March 2017 , August 2017

Descriptive Summary

Creator:	Hanna, Kathleen, 1968-
Title:	Kathleen Hanna Papers
Dates [inclusive]:	1988-2015
Abstract:	Kathleen Hanna was an early instigator of the Riot Grrrl Movement, performing in bands such as Bikini Kill and Le Tigre. The Kathleen Hanna Papers consists of flyers, posters, zines and zine masters, notebooks, ephemera, photographs, media, newspaper clippings, theses and other academic writing, and legal and financial records. The collection documents Hanna's artistic production, participation in the Riot Grrrl movement, curatorial work, and musical career.
Quantity:	7 Linear Feet in 10 document cases, 1 flat box, 2 binders and 1 oversize box
Language:	Materials are in English.
Call Phrase:	MSS.271

Messenger

Julie   Home

Messenger

30/01/2013 13:04

Sorry to do this, but I'm crowd sourcing for a project I'm working on--a project whose deadline is fast approaching.. Can you all reply to this, or to me personally, and tell me in a sentence or two: what's your take on feminism in the archive era? I'm asking this in wake of the Pussy Riot book, the Riot Grrrl archive, books on punk rock, more young (i.e. third wave) feminists in the academy.... If you have five minutes to give me your briefest thoughts, I'll love ya for it. (Feel free to reply in as a great a length as you'd like.. But for my purposes, I'm only asking for a little bit.) And if you are so inclined, you can certainly forward the question to whomever you'd like--even boys!

Thanks all! I really, really, really appreciate it!
--Julie

Just to clarify: you take "feminism in the archive era" to mean whatever you'd like, but I see it, in case that helps you think about it, as a current thrust in feminism that seems to be most interested in archiving feminism's histories/achievements.

↗ You added

↗ You added   and 2 others.

30/01/2013 17:19

Mimi

Hey Julie,

Type a message. @name...

Options

Q   Search in Conversation

✎   Edit Nicknames

🎨   Change Colour

👍   Change Emoji

🔔   Notifications

People

Rayna: i'm not sure i know what the archive era is

           i also haven't taken a feminist theory class in like
           5 years, so maybe this is something everyone is
           debating that i just don't know about

me: it's when the thrust of feminism seems to be archiving
           feminism's achievements/histories

Rayna: ohhh ok

           that makes sense

           is this something that is mostly an issue in feminism,
           or is it something that people are talking about across
           the board?

           like in other forms of activism

me: i think they're talking about it in other forms of
           activism too

           there is a course this semester about black power and
           the archive

Rayna: oh yeah, Orange and Purple are taking it

me: i thought about taking it but it seemed really similar to
           the black power course i just took

           anyway, i think it's a larger question

Rayna: so it's kind of related to or a reaction against the
           debates about being "post" everything?

           post feminist, post race, etc?

me: umm, i'm not really sure

            i think of it as being a question of is this still activism?
            or is activism being put into a museum, like it's part of
            the past now

            it's also a question of posterity

Rayna: oh ok

me: which is very important

            but yeah, i'm not sure what all the terms of the debate are

Rayna: ok i guess it sounds related to the postfeminism issue
            because it's asking whether the only way the feminist
            movement can still be relevant is by talking about its
            own past

            (like implicitly because there's a perception that there's
            nothing left to do, or no way to do it, in the present)

            or maybe that talking about the past is the only way to
            do something in the present

me: i think it's an interesting idea

            i feel like it's part of our moment, at least as far as
            activism is concerned

            at one point in its history, feminism moved into the
            academy. i feel like at this point, it's moving into
            the archive.

            but yeah, like you said, that doesn't mean it has to
            stay there.

FEMINISM IN THE ARCHIVE ERA

I am browsing the Feminist Archives.
The university libraries house them in their central middle-of-
    nowhere branch.
I heard about this place through graffiti on a bathroom stall.
Good thing I have all this menstrual blood to write with to fill out
    the call slips
because there's no money in the budget for little pencils.

Lonely on the margins
or lost in the middle
or nowhere at all.

Every archive is a radical act.
Every archivism is an act of radicalism.
Every activism is a radicalism.
Every archive is an activism that is radical.
Every radicalism is an archivable activism.
Every radical act is an archivable act.
Every archivable act is a radical act.
Every act of radicalism is an active archive.
Every radical act belongs to our archive.
Every utterance put on paper is an archive.
Our bodies are radical archives of activism.

Insist that new thought be produced through research.
Have capacious ideas of what research is.
Discover things that we hadn't expected,
that will fundamentally change what we think.
Make a positive and pleasurable centre.
Create poetry.

Description as experimental act that creates writing in relationship to
THE OUTSIDE WORLD!
This is a moment of expression!
Throw out phenomenology!
Or keep it but screw it!
Ask: Is this an I/You/Me/We that is happening right now?

Latin was the language of hegemony
and empire and now English is.
From now on I tell everything my way.

NOTES ON BIG DAN'S PRESENTATION ON THE FEMALE POET

- About presence of art in daily life
- Syllables, connected to rhythm & metre
- Prose poem and the grammar of the sentence
- Gentleman collector
- Display them in cabinets
- Syllables and sentences
- She says on page 97
- Uses the "We,"
- Unpacking those discourses
- Let's turn to page 19
- History, Architecture, Utopia
- V. beautiful
- Politics or ornamentation?

BIG DAN'S PRESENTATION ON THE FEMALE POET

Surface vs. structure and gendered understanding of that valuations of ornamentation, e.g. the vase of page 89 ties ornament to Capitalism. Joshua Clover wrote about her she's thinking about Capitalism assembly of and textual matter in what ways are her poems 3-D page 13 frustration with language refusal of expenditure in Bourgeois society, esp. according to Bataille (pushing back against Hegel) thinking about the non-recoupable Potlatch her use of *or* as a kind of synecdoche for *ornament* talking abstractly and imposing ideas on the text *ors* of page 90 reconnecting re-ornamentation and rhetoric research-based and experimental one mode BIG DAN I DON'T LIKE WHAT YOU TRY AND DO TO MY IDEAS expects to be lauded for revealing things in the past virtuous

A RESPONSE TO BIG DAN

Ummm

Um um ummm

Ummm umm

Uuuuuummmmmm

Umumumumumumum

...

Mmmmmmmuumumumum

...

um

um

um

um

um

um

...

(AHHHHHHH!)

THE YOUNG FEMINISTS MEET AN OLD FEMINIST

Big Dan is sitting next to me at the public library, clearing his throat and reciting page numbers aloud. He writes on a small folded paper and it becomes covered in numbers that are written in his shaky handwriting. His blue baseball cap says *USA* in a large yellow font.

Encyclopedia of New Jersey.
171
174

I am trying to write about yesterday, talking with Kate Millett and Simone de Beauvoir. With a group of feminists, most young, but one who lived the civil rights era, who had first-hand anecdotes of the hotly contested material that 1960s feminists were engaging with and disseminating. She told us about the danger in releasing this information, and the difficulty in calling yourself a feminist. And maybe it is because we are poor, but we understood how she felt.

745
36
35
Find it in the *Bible for Women.*

The room thinned out when the old feminist finished her presentation. A group of us, all young feminists (one white woman, one Puerto Rican woman, one gay white man, one straight black man) stayed behind to talk to her. She laughed and said she was giddy to have this conversation. How long had it been, we wondered, since she'd encountered students who loved literature for the politics? Who saw its connection to the conflicts and realities in our daily lives?

Heavy sigh: "I'm going to take these"
174
173
Brooklyn's Gold Coast
Zee
Double-you

We were giddy too. We'd found a mentor, at last, although she was nearing retirement, no longer taking on students for

87
87
And one dash

reading lists or dissertation supervision. She told us about a class she taught "a hundred years ago," she said. The readings were compiled by the members of the class, grades were determined by throwing a dart at a dartboard. Students and instructors read widely and wildly. It was her favourite course, one she remembered even a hundred years later. "Read it all. Read it because it's important to you."

159
158
ISBN 978-0802134844

The O books.
You can bring your coffee in here, as long as your cup has a lid. Water's fine. No food though.

EMOTION OF HOPE

RELATIONSHIP TO RELATIONSHIPS

She comes to the podium: "I want to be intimate with men. I do not desire that my relationships and my intellectual creative spaces be filled with women only. I am currently trying, for the first time in my life, to have an honest, committed, monogamous, adult relationship with a man I love who loves me too. I want to thank him for sharing his life with me. I've never felt so alive, so productive, so OKAY. I want for him to be part of the conversation. He deserves to be here. We are made better when he is included."

Q AND A

She stands up in the audience, walks to the microphone for the Q and A: "Oh! Boo hoo! Poor you! Boo hoo! Well, welcome to the real world, Sweetie Pie Two-lips. Welcome to your cunt and all its fucking pleasures!"

THE ARCHIVAL AGE

From inside the feminist bookstore: "But wait," she says, "I want
to talk about silence. Does dishing out the same *shut up* that we've
heard for so long make us more powerful? Are we trying to just
spread oppression more equally, thus begetting a new, morbid
equality? Are we all in this pit together? Maybe I should be
silent on this, or write it down in menstrual blood and delete the
pronouns. I'll fuck my sister, keep it in the family. Rainbows will
explode out our eyes when we cum. I could sink a ship, a big fat
cargo ship, a motherfucking oil tanker, with all my lust. But desire
should be a weapon – right? – pointed at the horizon, the one we
rode away from? That's where I should keep my anger and my
agency. Is that what you're saying?"

IMAGE CULTURE

At the tattoo parlour, she says: "My apartment is full of cockroaches. Yesterday, I started painting at one in the morning. First the washing of the walls, then the masking off and removing outlet covers. I walk under ladders because I DON'T CARE ABOUT THE FUTURE! I talk to my parents no more than once a week because I DON'T BELONG TO ANYONE!

There is a mudslide coming. A shitstorm. The radiators have been knocking for hours, like the bowels of this building are scheming, coming up with a plan. It's 2012. I keep hearing again that it's all over this time. But I only just met him. It hasn't been enough time, to feel his kneecaps against the backs of my knees while we sleep. Sitting on a too-small couch. Reading side by side. Sharing our prescription anti-anxiety drugs. Our cats were just starting to get along. And then, too soon, when we were only just beginning, we will suddenly be turned into nothing."

Thurston Moore and Kim Gordon split. Sonic Youth to follow.

NO THEORY

My scalp is bloody on the inside, and after that is hard bone
and then my thoughts and feelings. It's unlikely these soft and
hard things will not be messy. I recently started a knitting club.
Between that and my organic garden, my days are full – full
of purity and homemadeness – but I must send, with deepest
regret, this response to say that I cannot make it to your protest
today. And I would also like to say that my DivaCup is leaking,
but I use it anyway because tampons contain dioxins, no matter
what the corporations say, and nothing is so absorptive as a
woman's vagina, and I don't know what else to do, so I bleed
on my underwear. I avoid intimacy at these times, as well as at
others. Although I mostly date men, I was with a woman once,
but I don't talk about it much and I am reluctant to call myself
bisexual, or even bi-curious, because I worry that others will
think I'm pretending to be queer for attention, and so probably
I'm participating in bi-erasure – I do worry about that a lot –
but what does it mean to *me* that I was with a woman? And why
do I hide from the memory of it? Like, why does it feel shameful
to think about it? I thought I knew better than all that, but it's
like I don't know anything at all.

But

sometimes

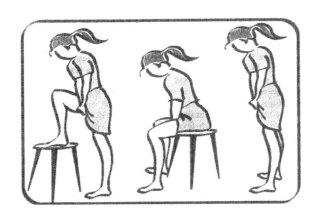

NO THEORY

I eat soft fruit when it's overripe, and I dig the meat of it away
from the pit with my tongue while my lips are pressed against
the soft, gritty texture of the skin, and then my fangs pop out
with arousal, and I tear and gnaw at the flesh until juices splatter
all over my face, even up my nose, and there is a moment or two
before I realize what I've done, and I think that during that time
the inside of my body swells like it is getting larger than my
skin, and I feel. But then I cannot get to a napkin fast enough,
and I look around to see if anyone saw, and I am back inside
my normal body.

NO THEORY

I don't have a lot of money, but I used what was left on my line of
credit to buy solid-gold grills. There is a small diamond on each
fang. And now storm clouds are rolling in. I want to buy another
cappuccino, so I can stay sitting under this awning, but I spent all
my money on grills. Tonight, I am planning to clean out the fridge
since it is garbage night. My video is due back tomorrow, and I
still haven't watched it. I might make a profile on ALT.com. I know
that so far, this day has been uneventful. I'm tired of deciding
that tomorrow will be better. I want more light than the glow of
refrigerators and computer screens. I want the blood in my veins
to turn black and boil, to have my gooey thoughts and sharded
feelings pour out my eyes and nostrils onto my lap, where I can
then spoon them back into my mouth and taste them, edgy and
burning, and I can digest them on my own, without having to look
at them or to know them at all. They will make their way through
my intestines and into my stomach, and there'll be nothing left at
the end of my neck but a deflated face.

NO THEORY

I have a tattoo on my neck of a dragon. It is designed to look as though I have a gash in my neck and out of that, a mythological beast is bursting forth. Most people, when they see it, have to ask what it is. My artistic vision is thwarted by my two-dimensional flesh. But trust me, I have a heart hidden deep beneath this irony.

FROM THE FIELD

Incident Report: White smudges on the couch in front of the bay window are indeed proof of exhibitionist masturbation.

Incident Report: Armpit stubble becomes increasingly visible after you leave the house.

Incident Report: Some people choose to give themselves a pedicure before they get a pedicure in order not to embarrass their feet.

Incident Report: The bicycle works just fine; you *choose* not to ride it.

Incident Report: He claims to have a gluten intolerance; yet, he eats cake often.

Incident Report: I'm on the streetcar. Just bought some cat food.

Incident Report: Her boss hides cocaine, precut, on a dessert plate inside the drop ceiling.

Incident Report: She's realizing the sketch she made that was meant to become a painting will soon itself be the finished product.

WE ARE FUN. PEOPLE LIKE US.

We just finished the angel food cake and now we're playing Cranium. I've confused two of the artisanal cheeses and presented the white cheddar as firm goat's cheese by accident. We have wine. We open a bottle we've been dying to try. We like the label.

We are working through things. Together. We talk about our problems. We blame our parents and not each other. We see therapists separately, maybe one day together. We have dinner parties. We buy expensive cheeses and cheap furniture and play board games with other couples. We have single friends, but they can't come for dinner because they screw up the symmetry and the math. I have six placemats, six matching big plates and six matching small ones. We tell jokes. We make fun.

The scene changes. Three couples are in a Brooklyn apartment, playing board games. The host has bought a variety of artisanal cheeses. The guests have all brought wine. My husband and I bring a rosé that we've been dying to try. We aren't bored yet of being in a routine.

It's our turn at the board game. Each couple forms a team. My husband and I select a category called humdinger. "I'd sure like a humdinger," he says, then puts his arm around my shoulders.

Another couple plays next. She is supposed to draw something with her eyes closed and he has to guess what it is. She scribbles a mess of lines on the paper, circling and circling, darker and darker. The time runs out, and he hasn't guessed.

"What is it?" he askes.

"A black hole," she says.

We all stare into the black hole.

"Yes, I see it," my husband says.

We all put our keys in a jar and then take off our clothes. We sit in
a circle looking at each other's naked bodies. Like an orgy without
touching. Our flesh is just a picture of flesh. There are cum stains on
the white carpet, but we'll never find them.

"The beginning of poetry is the origins of piracy," I say. "I won't anymore
live in a world where paranoia's the only possible act of knowing."

THE

ORANGE

TOXIC

EVENT

Now it starts being hard again.
Is this the end of irony?
The moment that I have been waiting for?
How arrogant of me.

We watched the election returns with certainty, and then we
realized that what we knew – in our hearts and minds – was
completely and totally wrong.

We coolly celebrated a woman president – one we did not like, a
war hawk with allegiance to the oligarchy – but come on, America,
you are so much more racist and sexist than I thought you were!

Sad![1]

That only means I wasn't listening.
My whiteness was blindness.
I observed activism moving into the archive and I was deaf
to POC citizens,
the systematically oppressed
who knew that the moment for activism
had not passed

who I claimed to have been an ally to
who I wrote to and with
I am ashamed
and afraid
and please, please, please, don't anyone come to my rescue.

White women voted for Trump.

---

[1] And see! I cannot let the irony away from me! It is part of me, even as it
makes me sick!

DIGITAL SPACE VERSUS WHAT HAPPENS ON PAPER

an image of Klimt
as disaster/freedom graffiti
beauty and the image
turns out to be not real, but not nothing at all

       how do you cultivate curiosity in the Internet age?
writers at work don't know how to answer that question
pictures of writers
at work
paper, desks, solitary
for them, information is scarce
for them, the goal is mastery
heavy heads hang in their hands

we live in a network-centric paradigm
put that in your pocket and don't think about it again until we're done
      talking if we're alone, then we are alone together

an image of Lee Miller in Hitler's bathtub
      how would you work backwards from a photograph?

for us, information is ubiquitous
and mastery no longer means mastery of content
for us, primacy is resourcefulness
and expertise should be generative rather than authoritative

down with vigilantism
up with multiple voices

WHAT DOES CULTURAL RESISTANCE LOOK LIKE?

One time, he asked me how I was doing. And I said "good," but I was
   supposed to have said "well."
So that's what it *sounds* like.
But what does it look like?

Since we are going to have to start taking for granted that if it's going to
   be resistant, it's going to also have to be a lot of other things too
AT ITS WORST and AT THE VERY LEAST
        then we can start to get a sense of what it looks like.

It probably hates capitalism –
        although it also likes to buy the things it needs and wants –
so we can suspect that it makes its own clothes.

It wears the brightly coloured balaclavas of freedom
        (from identity, from the male gaze)
and not the black masks of terrorism.

You can try and archive it
but it breaks out.

It lives in the streets.
Its feet and hands are dirty with urban silt.

Do we know yet what it looks like?
Because it has to look
and look like something
to get out there.
To get its message across.

Do you want an audience?

CUT AND PASTE

if you can cut and paste
you can do virtually everything

if you can customize
and upload
and surround with words
and upload
and attend
then

and then it rains
and you're almost washed away

THE FUTURE

Higher Education
Composing
      image
      text
      maps
           interactive
           self-generated
           online archive
                 modify the archive
                 add to the archive
                 build an archive
                      Composing

we all had our manual typewriters
our musical instruments

show us what's possible
when we move online

violation of house style
we do not allow ornamentals
we do not allow white space
or, we have all the white space you could want
or perhaps *or* is synecdochic of the ornamentals that we do not allow

How have we been prepared to thrive
in a world where writing has been redefined?

Exemption may not tell us what we think it tells us
Exemption maybe tells us what we think it tells us

Occupy this form with your content

SONNET

Banging steps up to the side door
Hockey in the back driveway
Uncle holds back the dog so he doesn't chase the ball
Elderly couple in matching blue shirts
Garages bigger than my apartment
Pink flowerpot next to a dead tree
A plastic tricycle out with the trash
"Ry" & "Ryder," he shouts

And finally, Volta red tulips!
There's a lot of pink – a milk crate, also pink plastic
Bundles of dead branches at the front of the yard look like a sculpture,
    a nest, a witch's spell
My apartment is bigger than I claim – I have my own office and a
    storage closet
The dog got the ball – I didn't mean to say mean things. What do you
    mean when you say I mean to say mean things?
A three-wheeled stroller pushed by a striped shirt and two Blue Jays.

SONNET

This is my new form of sonnet / This is the closing of it
                                                    — BERNADETTE MAYER

Intro: I have been interested in the situationists for a long time but haven't studied them in depth. There's been no burst of intense research, just small collections and gleanings of factoids. I like the idea of *détournement*: it feels really right to me. I read a book once about the situationists by McKenzie Wark, who once had a short romance with Kathy Acker. Some people think I should name my baby McKenzie, but that's too Park Slope. Psychogeography means laying a map over a physical space – a map and a space that do not logically or rationally correspond. This forms a kind of stretched comparison. Park Slope is like Leslieville if your map and your psycho- can align to make the same geography. You should walk in pairs. So that you stay focused on the walk instead of thinking about your mortgage, or the fact that you're too broke to ever really have a mortgage, or the fact that you do like the name McKenzie.

Sonnet:
Steps to side door
Backyard hockey
Holds back dog
Elderly couple
Garages
Pink flowerpot
A plastic tricycle
& "Ryder"

Finally, Volta red tulips!
There's a lot of pink plastic
Dead branches
My apartment is bigger than I claim
Dog got the ball
Three-wheeled stroller

Addendum: I was going to sit on a stranger's porch to write this down, to make their private property into a space of poetic production. I don't really believe in private property, which is infinitely easier since I have no money. One time I masturbated in an elevator just to prove that I could. Except I was too nervous and couldn't climax. In my dream I was waiting for the bus. Once I dreamt I was folding laundry. I gave my boss my phone number in case he needed me to work on Tuesday, and he winked at me. Some Mormons were in our neighbourhood on Saturday and they skipped my house and I was mad! What's wrong with my house? My boss and the Mormons are not in my dreams. They are real life.

FOURTEEN WORDS:

Blue Trilogy Flaxen Sunflower Pinwheel Carp Kamikaze
Maximum Parrot Free Walk Leather Refrigerator Blood

The Blue Trilogy centres too much on the flaxen-haired, on the
sunflower girls eating pinwheel sandwiches on the hot beach,
far from the bloated carp who wash up downstream after some
unknowable kamikaze mission. These girls parrot each other's
opinions and agree that university could never be free and they
hate to walk because what would their cars do without them?
Dear Reader, try instead the Red Trilogy, bound in leather, sitting
on top of the refrigerator, soaked in blood.

SONNET: FOURTEEN LINES

green grocers
greens (spinach)
strawberries (organic)
blueberries (if organic)
red pepper
onion (sweet)
brussels
broccolli
mushrooms
if they have honey crisp apples
get a couple
2 sweet potatoes organic
4 large red potatoes

We are out of ink.
magenta

I green grocers your lips
And would want to greens spinach your tongue
You strawberries too much (organic)
You blueberries in ways that forget me (if organic)
I red pepper in your veins
I onion when I'm not tired (sweet) (hypnogogic)
We might brussels together, later
When I broccoli and you notice
And you mushrooms in response
If they have honey crisp apples
We get a couple(d)
Too sweet when he potatoes organic like the rest
For large and red, I could potatoes too.

We are out of ink, Magenta.
(So how can we potatoes this poem?)

HE'S A STEPPIE SHARKS KIND OF GUY

I think I've been masturbating too much. It started years ago, and now that I'm getting old (probably most people think I'm in my mid-thirties, but really, I'm over sixty) it's still going on. I thought I'd have outgrown it by now.

I sometimes wonder if regular people have the problems that I do. Then I remember that they do not.

What I enjoy most is masturbating at work. I love to fantasize about the women I work with, some of whom are really just girls. They are teenagers, just out of high school, and they're working over the summer to get experience or just money for college. Actually, they are the ones I fantasize about the most. I especially like to imagine that I'm having sex with them in the work bathroom and my aid comes in and catches us just as she's orgasming and she yells out, "Yours is the biggest red button!" I think about this while I'm in the men's room stall, jerking off into the toilet. I jerk off four or five times a day. By number three or four, I've really got to jerk it, so my hand is gripped so tightly and moves so fiercely that I end up with a large sweat stain under my left armpit (I'm left-handed) and my face is red and sweaty with overexertion. Perhaps people think I go to the bathroom to cry? If that's what they think, they will certainly hear from my lawyers one day very soon.

The office isn't that big, kind of a dump in many ways, but it's big enough. Big enough that one guy can masturbate up to five times a day while at work, and this can go on for over a year, and no one seems to notice or care.

I'd say there are eighteen women in my office whom I fantasize about regularly. Some of the women I work with are in their thirties and not particularly attractive. I think about having sex with them in their small offices, coming up from behind them. They don't even know I'm there until I hoist up their skirt, pull down their stockings and underwear, and then smoothly enter their flabby, thirty-year-old pussy without even needing their guidance. They are surprised at first and would like to stop me, but I'm too quick, and by the time I'm thrusting and reaching around to grab their large but unfirm breasts, they are in such ecstasy that they never want it to stop. Perhaps I picture taking these women from behind because I ultimately find them so unattractive? I once thought that having sex with a woman from behind, even if it was in her pussy and not in her ass, meant that you were gay. I think that it does mean that for some men. I wonder if one day I will start to fantasize about men? Very attractive, successful men only, obviously. Certainly, that would make it easier to fuck in the gender-segregated work washrooms.

Some of the women I work with are chubby. Many of them are in their forties or even fifties. They chain-smoke, some of them. One woman smokes about two packs a day. I imagine fucking her out by the smoking pit, with the water-damaged picnic table acting as an impromptu bed. Once, I imagined that one of the women was smoking the whole time I was fucking her. Both her hands were clawing my back while the cigarette perked up between her lips, not so much dangling as being held erect. Later, I thought again about signs that I might be gay. Was the cigarette not a symbol of a penis? Especially since, in my fantasy, this cigarette insisted on being so erect?

There is one woman I work with whom I fear I am falling in love with. She is about twenty-five, maybe twenty-six or twenty-seven. She got married last year and the heavy rings on her left ring finger make me chubby. I've been fantasizing about her since she started working here four months ago. She is the most regular, consistent fantasy that I have. I avoid talking to her since I fear that my voice or gestures would inadvertently give me away. Perhaps she would sense that I am the kind of guy who masturbates five times a day at work. Perhaps she would know that she holds a special place in my stable of fantasies. Or she may also reveal a tic – something I haven't noticed from a distance. Something off-putting or rank. I like all kinds of women, as I think I've made clear. Still, I don't want to lose my number one fantasy girl to some irritating trait that will forever soften my penis. I can't imagine what that trait could be – but that's just the point! I don't want to know, even in my imagination!

There are a couple of ways that I like to intensify my fantasies: One is that I like to imagine getting the girls pregnant. Not the older women, but the teenage girls especially. They are about to start college, but I imagine that I knock them up and they have to tell their parents that they can't go to college because actually, they're pregnant by the red-faced guy at work. I don't imagine us spending our lives together or raising the kid together. I just imagine the girls with big, round baby bellies and sad eyes. And I fuck them in the washroom at work, just like before, only this time they are more desperate and give in way more easily because they figure once they have a baby at age eighteen, then no one is going to want to fuck them again.

These are just fantasies. The teenage girls work in another part of the office, not in the main part, where I am. I see them when they come into work in the morning, go out for lunch and come back from lunch, and then when they leave in the evening. Sometimes I don't see them come or go because I'm in the washroom masturbating.

Another thing that helps me intensify my fantasies is that I like to think about cumming inside of women's shoes, or, as I like to call them, their steppie sharks. Some women have steppie sharks that they leave at the office. Either heels for when they meet clients, or slipper-like steppie sharks instead of boots in the winter. Or maybe they just like a change? Women have a thing with steppie sharks, I know that. I think that's why I like steppie sharks so much. I feel like they're something that women see as an extension of themselves. Part of their feet, but also part of their sexiness, part of their womanliness. That's the shark part. I like to think about fiercely stroking my dick until cum splatters into the toe of their steppie sharks. I also imagine them putting their steppie sharks on, not suspecting that I have masturbated with them and cum inside, and then wondering what is on their foot. They would feel it on their bare feet and even through stockings. I really enjoy thinking about the toes of a woman's stockings covered in my jizz, sticking rudely to her toes, and her staring at the mess, absolutely perplexed, thinking *what the heck could that be?* Maybe they would wonder if they had stepped in hair gel, or cake frosting. Then they would decide to forget about it and go back to work, and my cum would stay stuck to their stockings or their toes and shoved back inside their pretty steppie shark.

I must confess, this part of my masturbation routine is more than just fantasy. I have recently begun to take steppie sharks from the shared office spaces where the women leave their extras. I sneak them out of their little corners, tucked away but not entirely hidden, and then I bring them into the bathroom stall with me. I absolutely fill their steppie sharks with my semen! I sometimes have enough to do more than one shoe at a time! And then I think fondly, so lovingly and fondly, about them putting their steppie sharks on the next day, their bare feet covered in my semen.

Since the spare steppie sharks are not always left near a person's desk, I often can't identify whose steppie sharks are whose. I have my suspicions: Chubby women in their fifties do not wear high heels, I don't think. And my girl – my twentysomething, married, number one fantasy girl – I suspect, has a thing for neutral colours, and so her steppie sharks are often beige or grey. Still very patent, very sexy, tall heels with slender, pointed toes. But tastefully neutral. I love the sound of clicking steppie sharks on the office floor. It is the sound of beautiful, young women.

I choose the neutral-coloured heels most often. I only started this phase of my masturbation habit in the last few weeks. No one knows about this, but it wouldn't matter if they did. They are just fantasies. I'm just really into women, and really into steppie sharks. And there's nothing else to say.

I HATE THE COUNTRY I RULE

I hate the country
I rule
Fat fingers reaching for dollar bills
Exploding out of oil barrels
Refined by boys from Ontario
Who now live in Alberta.

Born in the country I hate
I will not tolerate
Even the dreamers
They are gone gone gone

I hate you dyke-march assholes
With your bare breasts and
Your bicycles.

I hate taxes
And government
And ugly ladies
And crooked Hillary
And black people
And Mexican rapists
And homos

I hate voting and elections.
I hate the opposition and erections.
The jury's out on those ice caps –
Are they melting?
Nah, they're just teasing.
I hate evolution
And science
And libraries.
I hate the country
I rule.

Quebec: "Boo hoo!"
Natives: "Boo hoo!"
Artists: "Boo hoo!"
Women: "Boo hoo!"
Women: *grabby grabby mee-ooww*

Grow up and double-peck
Each cheek
Of the Queen
Of the Commonwealth
And maybe one day
You'll get your very own
Hockey jersey!

(Secretly, I miss you, Jack.
Not a day goes by that I don't think of your moustache,
your cane,
your socialism.
In these moments,
not even Laureen can comfort me.
I go inside myself
and I cry for those burned books,
that trade deal with China,
old people,
all the unemployed mail carriers.
All my errors; all we've lost.)

Grow up and see who the real fake crooks are
The media foxes who slither away from my Truth
– Steve! Mike! My cappuccino! –

(Barry, you are everything to me, and you know you always have been.
You are in my mind when I wake up,
when I change my hair,
when I wash my teeth,
through the whole shithole day.
It is you I think about,
Barry.

Your words and your magic seduced and terrified me and –
I think you know this already –
you became my obsession.
And I am shrinking from your memory and your legacy.
My hands are going first,
next my teeth,
my eyes,
not my dick,
never my dick,
my feet,
and on and on and on.

Mel hates me for it.
She hates me for so much.
And I can't blame her, since it's you,
Barry,
it's always been you.
My heirs will know, as she does, that they were born into a shadow
and they will know better than me – since none can know worsely –
how to be in such a shadow. How not to lose yourself,
or to become yourself,
and they will know which is harder,
and which is worsely.) *

---

* (No, fool, we will hang them. They will know you as a torturer and a
tyrant, as we do. They will flee to shithole countries, hoping for safety there,
but all we can promise them is vengeance. And it will be in your name.
And that is the name your friends and heirs will scream as they perish in
our new and better world.)

THE SUICIDAL REVOLUTIONARIES, OR GOD BLESS KATHY ACKER

It was at this time that the student revolutionaries, more professionally armed than any of the cops around them, burst into the English Embassy, which was located next to the slum. Though paying in serious injury and death, they successfully demolished the government building.

KATHY ACKER
Pussy, King of the Pirates

In those days, there were too many bodies for there to be such a thing as murder.

KATHY ACKER
Pussy, King of the Pirates

LE CARRÉ ROUGE

They shut down our chances, made curfews, warned us to stay indoors. "Women will be raped," they said. "Children will be killed and eaten. Men will have their wallets stolen." We had no time for these threats. We were desperate to fuck, to be killed and eaten, and none of us knew what a wallet even was. We stuck our fingers up our cunts, spread a red square of menstrual blood across our chests, and we took to the streets. We blurred together there, like a painting, a canvas dripping and swirling, that wouldn't dry. There were cops with plastic guards over their faces, with helmets and clubs. We sprayed them with ylang-ylang, a well-known aphrodisiac. Nothing. They stood their solid, fascist ground, oinking and digging their hooves into the hot asphalt.

PRISONS

I cried real tears. My friend spat on the ground, on top of my tears, asserting that even in sadness there must also be anger. One of the oinking cops, reeking of aphrodisiac, said to her, "That is a six-hundred-dollar fine for spitting in public. Get in my car. I'm taking you uptown, then downtown, then to the suburbs for processing. I'm going to release you in America, where your money is no good. You can find your own way home. See how well that bloody chest will protect you then!" He laughed loudly and threw his head back. Since he wasn't looking, we ran into the crowd and disappeared, nameless again on the city street where we loved and slept and chalked and skipped and cried and spat.

It was at this time that the student revolutionaries, more professionally armed than any of the cops around them, burst into the English Embassy, which was located next to the slum. Though paying in serious injury and death, they successfully demolished the government building.

"These streets are ours!" my friend said, throwing a fist into the air. It rained, but our chests stayed bloody. Nothing was washed away.

THE SUMMER PROJECT

The news came on later that day, through my TV that wasn't even plugged in. It said there had been nine thousand people arrested in yesterday's protest. Only nine thousand and fifty people even lived in our town. *In those days, there were too many bodies for there to be such a thing as murder.* Everyone who was not a police officer was arrested. I sank into my sheets, lowering into my bed, into the floor, then into the basement. I waited there, buried in cement, a dead girl where no one would ever find me. I thought of teeth and lips and wondered where I would wake up tomorrow.

YESTERDAY AGAIN

My friend threw her fist into the air. "We'll go out fucking if the bastards come for us!" She fell hard on her knees, letting the blood from the torn skin pour out freely. "Suck what will one day be my scabs! Suck my scars-to-be!" We were with the other revolutionaries at last. We were bloody and confrontational. We cried and spat furiously, this time tears of joy, but still, as before, coated in angry spit.

NO MORE PRISONS

The government crumbled. We ate cake. We tongued each other's mouths. We took off all our clothes and burned them in the public square. We constructed entire buildings out of books. We only used concrete when we needed somewhere to write our graffiti. We mouthed and gestured. We vibrated and played. Skipping rope stopped being just for girls. We read aloud. We came together.

IT COULD BE WORSE

You could be naked.
You could have sickness.
You could bear children.
You could beget, be begotten.

IT COULD BE WORSE

You could snore, or have night terrors, or grind your teeth.
One leg could be shorter than the other,
both hands lost at war.
You could have a drinking problem.
You could be a Mennonite.

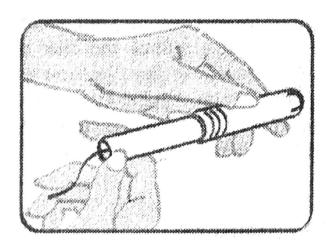

IT COULD BE WORSE

You could be a black hole, the source of endless quandary, fear,
    speculation.
You could be an orphan.
You could have a fever.
It could be raining.
What if you were allergic to sunlight?

IT COULD BE WORSE

You could be lactose intolerant.
You could have worked your entire life in print-based publishing.
Your throat could be closing, your eyes could be tearing.
You could be edible and your neighbours, hungry.
You could get nosebleeds.

IT COULD BE WORSE

Or what if you were born in Afghanistan?
What if your house had been built on a nuclear reactor?
And then there was a tsunami?
What if your family was a different species than you and had been
    poached and made into ashtrays?

IT COULD BE WORSE

You could be other than.
You could be un-American.
You could have been in the wrong place at the wrong time.
You could have accidentally killed your own dog.
You could have been hacked.
You could have waited all that time for nothing.
You could have cooked a dinner that tasted bad so you threw it
   out and ordered a pizza.

IT COULD BE WORSE

You could be really, really fat.
You could be a sophomore's party drink – consumed quickly,
    tastelessly, then thrown up.
You could have put your good gun rack out with the garbage.
You could have burned yourself.
You could have cut off the very tip of your finger.
You could bite your tongue.
Or paper-cut your cheek while licking an envelope.

IT COULD BE WORSE

Your eyes could have stayed like that.
That scar could have healed and then no one would believe you.
You could have forgotten the ending.
You could have hurt your back doing that.
You could have caught a cold.

IT COULD BE WORSE

You could iron a hole in your shirt.
You could get drunk before dinner.
You could forget.
You could have to apologize.
You could not be forgiven.
You could be forgiven.
You could lose it all.
And it might never come back.

IT COULD BE WORSE

Your neutral facial expression could look like a smirk.
You could have laughed inappropriately.
You could have died before you were born.
You could have been wounded in your face, your groin or your feelings.
You could have low self-esteem.

IT COULD BE WORSE

You could be hairless from the waist down.
You could have bought a bridge.
You could have formed a union.
You could have voted wrong.

IT COULD BE WORSE

You could bite your nails down to the quick.
You could die from sneezing or get the hiccups forever.
You could get so sick that you barf up your own testicles.

Or you could be you, you dumb piece of shit. You could be you.

HAIBUN DRIBS AND DRABS /
SCARS AND SCABS

AFTER BASHŌ'S "BRUSHWOOD GATE"

After nine springs & winters of a lonely, alcoholic life in the city,
I moved to the cheap and rugged coast of the Atlantic Ocean.
Someone once said, "Buy a guitar and learn how to play it." Is it
because I am poor myself that I can understand this feeling?

against feelings and words

expression went away

but it came back again

AFTER BASHŌ'S "LIVE AUSTERE AND CLEAR"

Lonely poverty, howling at the moon. Lonely poverty, lamenting holed shoes. Lonely poverty, dreaming about my one-woman show. Lonely poverty, no one responds and more lonely poverty.

"Live austere and clear!!!"

the werewolf performance artist's

beer-drinking song.

PUNK ROCK BOYS' CLUB

Imagining that boy is a girl and thinking of her with that same punk style. Shoulders, lips, stare. Eyeliner might be called ebony & sickness; midnight-dark sky; black hole of blackness; eternal nothingness. It would be burnt and then smudged like Courtney Fucking Love. And a leather jacket black as liquorice.

She only visited New York City once

and when she went

she didn't ask directions from anyone.

WHITE SMUDGES

The moment I noticed the scrunched-up Kleenex in the crack
between the cushions, I knew my boyfriend had masturbated on
the couch. White smudges on the fabric verified my suspicion.
There is no shame in masturbating, but why should I clean it up?
Just because I was too busy [blank]ing to screw?

In a cramped one-bedroom apartment

white smudges become

a blame machine.

LIST OF PLAUSIBLE EVENTS LEADING UP
TO THE TATTOO

This is a sound decision. I am a rugged individual. Steady line down the sidewalk. Boys and teething cream and India ink and sewing needle and thread and vodka and fatigue and Percocets and marijuana (no thanks) and nicotine (yes please).

Skinny arm

Shaky hands

Perforations

Heart-shaped

SUNRISE

The sun rises and I have been to bed. The sun rises before the coffee shops are open. The sun rises on my good health and happiness. What will I do today?

Forget loneliness.

Forget.

Loneliness.

POETRY

Within this D-prived skin and scarred lung cavities, there is
something. Sometimes I think of it as the image of me I want to
give or the image of me I want to see. Can we please just say it's
complex; serious, but with a wonderful sense of humour? It is fond
of drunkenness, self-abuse and precise vocabularies, and it made
these things its raisons d'etre. At times, sobriety has seemed viable,
as fatigue crept in and as therapy healed the desire for self-harm;
at times, it has gone too far, said too much, become the indulgent
excessiveness it most hates. It boasted of victories. Among these
hundred bones and billions of cells, it battles ceaselessly; it is
never at rest. It yearns for worldly success, but poetry keeps it real.
It educates and is educated, but it will not lose poetry. Without
talent or skill, it traces lines along lines like this one.

WORDS ON A COLD NIGHT

I live in love and comfort. My roof is not thatch. My floor is not mud. It is cold out my window. I gaze on the bare branches in the distance.

THE ELEGANT MEN

The elegant men swill their cups of lonely poverty and drink what to them is most delicious. They are ignored, but their delicate smiles face the sun. Their skin is gauze in the wind. They walk slowly, feeling every step.

EXCLAMATION POINT!

Start! Command! Change! Enable! When praise is real, we rarely exclaim it. We rest, steep, hold it still. We love in slow, backpedal motion. A thin blanket is no trouble. I live in comfort and love.

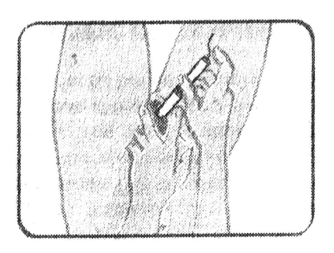

FIRE POEMS I

THE FIRST POEM: DESTRUCTION

We broke apart too suddenly, afterwards, all of us. We couldn't last through the shatter. I asked my mom what she thought, what she remembered. She said she only wanted no funeral.

My two eyes and your two legs, both fading, straining, snapping. My glasses, your cane: Either never strong enough to save a life. Neither ever strong enough to save a life.

I wish you'd talked more about Saskatchewan. I wish I knew about your mother, who only spoke Norwegian. I wish that I could speak Norwegian too.

I've heard that fire moves fast, and I thought I knew all about it. I thought I knew how fast fire moved, but now I think that I never knew, that only you know, but you aren't telling. You are not telling me about Saskatchewan, or about your mother, her Norway, or how fast fire moves. I would have given you my glasses, my strong prescription, because I think that strength may have helped you. I could have hoisted your cane. I was too far away. Even the phone call took too long to get to me. Fire moves faster than sound moves through copper wires.

When your house is on fire and you are in it, you should crawl on the ground. Smoke inhalation can kill you quickly. What I am about to say will make sense only to you, but given all the options presented to you when dying in a fire, I wish that you had died of smoke inhalation. I can't imagine burning. I would rather be asphyxiated. I wished that for you, but you were on the ground crawling, I heard, and the smoke couldn't reach you. You were right, again, always, I know; I listened to everything you said, quietly and stoically, trying to be just like you and I am still always trying to be just like you because I don't think that anyone else knows anything, not like we do. You did exactly what you were supposed to do and I don't know if it worked, or if you think that it worked. You did exactly what you were supposed to do and now you are dead from it. You are dead from doing exactly what you were supposed to do and you died in the worst way possible.

When your house is on fire, you should yell for your life because you are nearly engulfed in flames. This sounds funny, in a way, but I know that it would be hard for you to cry out, to cry for help. Did you try and *manage* something, as Aunt Susan would say? A burner that wouldn't light? A little spark that hit your synthetic bathrobe? A tea towel misplaced? That is the right time to cry for help, a gentle cry, but one that can still be heard. I would have done the same thing, you know; I would have tried to manage it on my own. It's what I am doing right now. I do it all the time. I wanted to call my mother, your daughter, to tell her that she was too stern, that I was too sad, but instead I sat right in the middle of my bed and then pressed my face against my pillow and yelled as loud as I could. We have all been given your stoicism, your dignity and grace, whether we asked for it or not.

Fire is impossible to photograph. Its power has nothing to do with stillness. Its powerful colour is not rendered on film because it doesn't really exist as a colour at all. It is the colour of heat, and you feel that colour on your skin and in your bones when you are close to a fire. You put your hands out and the colour of the fire hits your hands, and no one would know it was fire if they were looking at it through a lens. It would just be hands, reaching out, palms forward, like they were pressed up against nothing, no touch, but there would be, in fact, lots of touch. A touch that could destroy you.

You used to love sitting by the fire, at your trailer park, at those campgrounds, with your white wine and the tall trees all around you. The tall trees would sway and it was better than a ball game and we could watch it for hours, up close to the fire because you were always cold and always so sensitive to the fire and how hot it was getting, stoking or blowing, getting closer to it with your hands curled around logs, when your legs were strong. Then you would move back to your chair and watch the trees move back and forth in the sky. You sat so still and they moved all around us in a swaying circle. I had shorts on and the fire felt hot against my legs. Once, when I was a kid, I left my wet shoes too close to the fire and they melted, and still as a teenager, and still as a twenty-year-old, and still as a thirty-year-old, you reminded me not to leave my shoes too close to the fire or they would melt. Mistakes are not easily forgotten for you, or for my mother, your daughter, who also reminds me not to lose my glasses like I did when I was nine. I can't forget your mistake, either, of getting too close to the fire and trying to manage it on your own. This is a mistake that I know I will make too, no matter how many reminders I receive. I miss you every day.

I asked grandma if she believes in God. She said she does, but then she looked away and said it's heaven that she doesn't believe in, because there is nothing better than being alive on earth. I want you to be alive on earth.

Erica has your journals, which is a travesty. Erica is a dumb moron shit for brains. Every goddamned person here knows that they should be mine. Every motherfucking idiot with a pea brain in their head knows that I am the grandchild who ought to have those journals. But instead they're in her garage, losing their fire smell. She wants to make them into a digital file. I want to stick a pen in her throat. She said that you two both talked about it and that she wanted the journals and then she said – she motherfucking said! – that you wanted her to have them too and I do not believe a word of it. You wrote every day like I do. You kept it all in a book and in your head. Erica couldn't keep her mouth shut to save the whole world even if you were still in it. This is one more death. This is you dying a second time.

Uncle Joseph says that you would have had a stroke soon, so the fire was, in a way, a blessing. I know that if it weren't for the fire, then you would have lived for at least ten more years. You would have been at least ninety-three years old, even older. You were sharp still, smart about baseball scores and Rwanda and Harper and the Olympics, and you hated NASA and you voted NDP. You had the cane and the wobbly legs, but you were not ready to go; it was not your time, and your time wasn't even near. It was the wrong time. You were robbed and so were we all. I don't know what everyone is talking about. If the fire hadn't taken you, nothing would have.

FIRE POEMS II

PRELUDE

Fire is impossible to photograph. Its power has nothing to do with stillness. Its powerful colour is not rendered on film because it doesn't really exist as a colour at all. It is the colour of heat, and you feel that colour on your skin and in your bones when you are close to a fire. You put your hands out and the colour of the fire hits your hands, and no one would know it was fire if they were looking at it through a lens. It would just be hands, reaching out, palms forward, like they were pressed up against nothing, no touch, but there would be, in fact, lots of touch. A touch that could destroy you.

SCENE 1

Snow is falling gently on the stage. A row of fire hydrants or trees lines the front of the stage. They are all painted red. At the back of the stage on the right, there is a long hallway. At the back of the hallway is one chair, a plastic folding one probably purchased at Walmart or Ikea (read: cheap). The hallway is only wide enough to fit the chair. It is wallpapered from floor to ceiling with pink wallpaper. Along the ceiling of the hallway are a row of candelabras, all dimly lit.

Suddenly! three spots of light appear and dance around the part of the stage not occupied by the hallway. Like this:

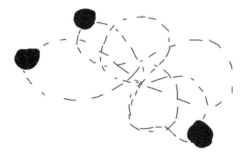

Suddenly! they stop.

Then they come together into one bright light.

They get brighter and brighter until they explode.
It continues to snow.
It is cold, but it has been colder.
Blackout.

SCENE 2

An actor walks across the stage.
Then exits.

Then they come back onstage, this time with a shovel, and begin
to remove snow from the stage, throwing it into the orchestra pit.
Eventually they uncover a door in the floor. They open the door
and pull out a wrench (a big, old one that looks like a murder
weapon) and a hammer and a saw and a typewriter. They set
the typewriter down at the front of the stage. Then they take the
hammer, saw and wrench and begin to dismantle everything
onstage except the hallway. Once something has been taken
apart, they pile the debris left from it into the hallway and then go
to the typewriter and type something onto a small piece of paper.
Then they place the piece of paper in the spot where the thing was.
When this is done, the stage is empty except for the writing and
the snow and the hallway, which is completely full of stuff so that
you cannot use it as a hallway. Some of the stuff catches on fire
from the candelabras. The actor rips off each of their fingernails
one at a time and puts them in a row on the stage. Then, where
each of their fingernails is grows a rose. This looks completely
beautiful in the middle of all the snow. The actor looks at the roses
and smells each one. Then they smile and walk to the hallway,
now completely on fire. They cannot leave and they cannot stay.
They are trapped where they are: In stasis. Unless they exit again.
But let's say that this is not an option.

Blackout.

SCENE 3: OURS

our bag
our handiwork
our coats
our thin and fragile
our lying
our two hands
our disappointment
our now

SCENE 4

It is snowing gently and rapidly on the stage, accumulating on the ground and forming a deep, dense carpet. Four actors enter stage left and walk single file along a path that spans miles and miles, already carved through the centre of the stage. Viewed from above, the actors look like glowing circles of light. They are joined by two other orbs, now making six as they traverse the snow, single file. When they finally reach a clearing, they form a circle and drop their backpacks to the ground. They pull out several logs of chopped wood, flasks of whisky, wrapped flanks of raw meat and extra scarves and blankets. They set to work building a fire and when it is done, all six sit around it in perfect symmetry. They place the meat on rocks just inside the fire's perimeter and watch it blacken. The fire finishes with the meat, then moves closer to the six actors. They sip on whisky flasks, of which they have only three, so they pass them around the circle. One of the actors starts singing a low, quiet song about living in the mountains, about not knowing flat land. The fire keeps moving outward, burning through the snow that is useless to contain it. It melts the rubber soles of the actors' winter boots. The heat continues to penetrate the rest of their clothing, peeling off jeans and then long underwear, down coats and wool sweaters, exposing bare skin to the harsh heat, then melting it down too. It bubbles and blackens and peels from their skeletons. Their bones begin to melt and drip like candle wax, running slowly down their long, vertical forms. Then they liquefy completely, making six wet holes in the snow. The puddles begin to boil as the fire moves closer. The fire touches them and they evaporate.

Blackout.

SCENE 5: WE

we had skinned it
we had feared the wind
we lay
We hoped
we must remain
we were
we would make ourselves
we quarried stone in the debris at the bottom
we had
we had
we worked
we had
we now kept at it until
we had finished
we closed the doorway
we could see we
afterwards
we were none
we had got our skin
we thought *existence*

SCENE 6

The curtain rises on a scene in progress. Snow is falling on trees. Their branches begin to slope and curve under the weight of the rapidly falling snow. The branches creak and bend until they almost touch the ground. Three actors walk along the snowy path, their eyelashes thick with white snow so that they almost cannot see their way. They have come from a nearby tavern after a night of drinking and singing and banging open palms on tabletops along with the beat of the music. They sit beneath a bent tree branch, taking shelter from the snow as it falls. Looking down from above, no one is there. From above, the tree branches do not appear to be bent. Looking at them this way, there is no worry that the bent branches will break. The snow keeps falling and piling on. The travellers sit and imagine a fire burning inside their little shelter and are immediately warmer. They hum the tune that is still in their heads.

Blackout.

SCENE 7: I

I was
I do not
I found my way
I strung up
I lasted
I am
I am
I will
not
I will
I am forever
I wrung my hands
I can
I'

SCENE 8

The actors were full of deep, burning energy. They felt their guts get
hot. They'd been told by their director to try harder, to participate
better. To professionalize. Their hands were blistered already.
Their eyes were dark and dry. Their lips were chapped and their
feet were throbbing. You've got to believe me, they'd given their all.
They each wept, quietly, ashamed to seem as though they couldn't
take this constructive criticism. Ashamed to be so weak and so
sensitive. They wiped away their tears and thought about icicles,
dazzling. They pictured the hot, white exhaust left behind planes
that crossed the sky. Each actor took a deep breath, feeling their
lungs soak into the back of their rib cage. They moved towards the
stage just as the snow began to fall.

Blackout.

SCENE 9

The reviews were fabulous. "More like reality than fiction," said one. "I know that they all have successful careers ahead of them," said another. The actors rubbed their insoles sitting around a fire they had built next to the snowy stage. They passed around champagne in mugs while the bottle sat chilling in a snow pile beside them. Their hands were blistered and bleeding. Their vision blurred from lack of sleep. Had it been worth it, they wondered, even after such strong reviews? They sipped their cold champagne and pulled their blankets around themselves tightly. The crisp air burned their noses, felt sharp in their lungs.

Blackout.

EPILOGUE

The actors all kept journals. They didn't care which book they used, so long as they could write in it every day. Some of them wrote overtop of the printed letters in novels, cookbooks, travelogues – pre-published material that they never read but had a vague sense they could improve upon. Some of the actors used bound sketchbooks, scrapbooks or planners, or anything they could find or were given. They wrote every day, recording the temperature, the laundry schedule, their partner's new haircut or the status of their broken watch. On the coldest days, their handwriting shook and wobbled. It could have been nearly impossible to read, should anyone have been meant to read it. On milder days, snow fell and wet the paper with small circles. Some days, tears fell from an actor's eyes onto the page, becoming indistinguishable from the larger snowflakes. The actors wrote together quietly at the same time every day. They held hands afterwards or sat quietly, still thinking but too tired to write. Their bodies were part of this paper and ink. They smiled at each other or just stared straight in front of them, knowing that this writing came from the body.

Blackout.

NOTES

Three of the poems from Young Love in the Post-Activism Era previously appeared in *TRANSverse Journal*.

The two paragraphs at the start of The Suicidal Revolutionaries, Or God Bless Kathy Acker are taken from Acker's novel *Pussy, King of the Pirates* (New York: Grove Press, 1996). The poems in this section of the collection appropriate and reimagine the text from these paragraphs. Quoted dialogue at the end of the poem "We Are Fun. People Like Us" is also taken from this book.

The poems in Haibun Dribs and Drabs / Scars and Scabs were inspired by and are indebted to *Bashō's Journey: The Literary Prose of Matsuo Bashō,* translated by David Landis Barnhill (New York: State University of New York Press, 2005).

ACKNOWLEDGEMENTS

This collection began in Sina Queyras' graduate poetry workshop at Concordia University. Without the inspiration and encouragement I received from all the members of the workshop, this collection likely wouldn't exist. They gave me the confidence to take this work seriously and to put it out into the world. Thanks especially to Laura Broadbent, Deanna Fong, Ben Hynes, Lise Gaston and, of course, Sina.

Many, many – so, so many! – thanks to the folks at Buckrider Books and Wolsak & Wynn, especially Noelle Allen and Ashley Hisson, who seem to be endlessly gracious, enthusiastic and supportive. To the kind, generous, talented and insightful Paul Vermeersch, who is not only a brilliant editor but also an exemplary citizen of the literary community. I'm proud to have worked with you.

Thanks to Ryan Rosler, Jayne Hildebrand and Atli Bollason – early readers of the collection who offered feedback and encouragement.

I am always thankful for the support of Katrina Best and Kasia Juno, fellow pirates, intrepid travellers and writer-friends from the beginning. Dear Reader, do yourself a favour and google them.

Every day and forever, I want to thank my sons, Reg and Frankie, and my hubby, Sean Springer. You guys are my rock. Thanks also to Sandy and David McIsaac, my A+ parents, who have given me everything. I won the birth lottery. Big time.

Deepest gratitude and honour to all the women in the Concordia University Creative Writing Program and the CanLit world who harnessed the #MeToo moment and took action against a toxic culture. The women who took no shit, who told their stories again and again, and who will change this culture for the better. You've inspired me and many others in ways you may never know. Smashing the patriarchy is too often thankless work, so let me take this time to say to you all, *thank you.*

IMAGE CREDITS

The images on pages 8, 17, 51, 72, 104 and 127 are from *Organyc: Organic Cotton Menstrual Tampons* (New York: CORMAN USA Inc.).

The image on page 25 is from Jenna Ashton, "Feminist Archiving [*a manifesto continued*]: Skilling for Activism and Organising," Abstract, *Australian Feminist Studies* 32, no. 91–92 (2007), https://www.tandfonline.com/doi/abs/10.1080/08164649.2017.1357010.

The image on page 27 is from "Guide to the Kathleen Hanna Papers, 1988–2015 MSS.271," The Fales Library & Special Collections, last modified August 2017, http://dlib.nyu.edu/findingaids/html/fales/hanna/.

The image on page 29 is from the author's Facebook account, January 30, 2013.

The image on page 31 was taken by the author on January 30, 2013, at Rutgers University Art Library, 71 Hamilton Street, New Brunswick, New Jersey, USA.

The image on page 77 is a shopping list found by the author in June 2015 on Logan Avenue, Toronto, ON, Canada.

JULIE McISAAC is a writer, artist, maker and momma with years of experience teaching writing at advanced levels. She's worked in Hamilton, Toronto, Montreal and New York City. While living in NYC, she hosted several salons in her home and loved bringing together creative people in informal spaces. That's one of the reasons she started hosting writing workshops in Hamilton. Her first book, *Entry Level*, was published with Insomniac Press in 2012. She lives in Hamilton, Ontario.